Anne Duval

Home Canning

and

Preserving

for beginners

A Complete step by step Guide.

Freezing, Drying, Canning and Preserving food in Jars

Copyright © 2020 publishing.

All rights reserved.

Author: Anne Duval

No part of this publication may be reproduced, distributed or transmitted in any form or by any means, including photocopying recording or other electronic or mechanical methods or by any information storage and retrieval system without the prior written permission of the publisher, except in the case of brief quotation embodies in critical reviews and certain other non-commercial uses permitted by copyright law.

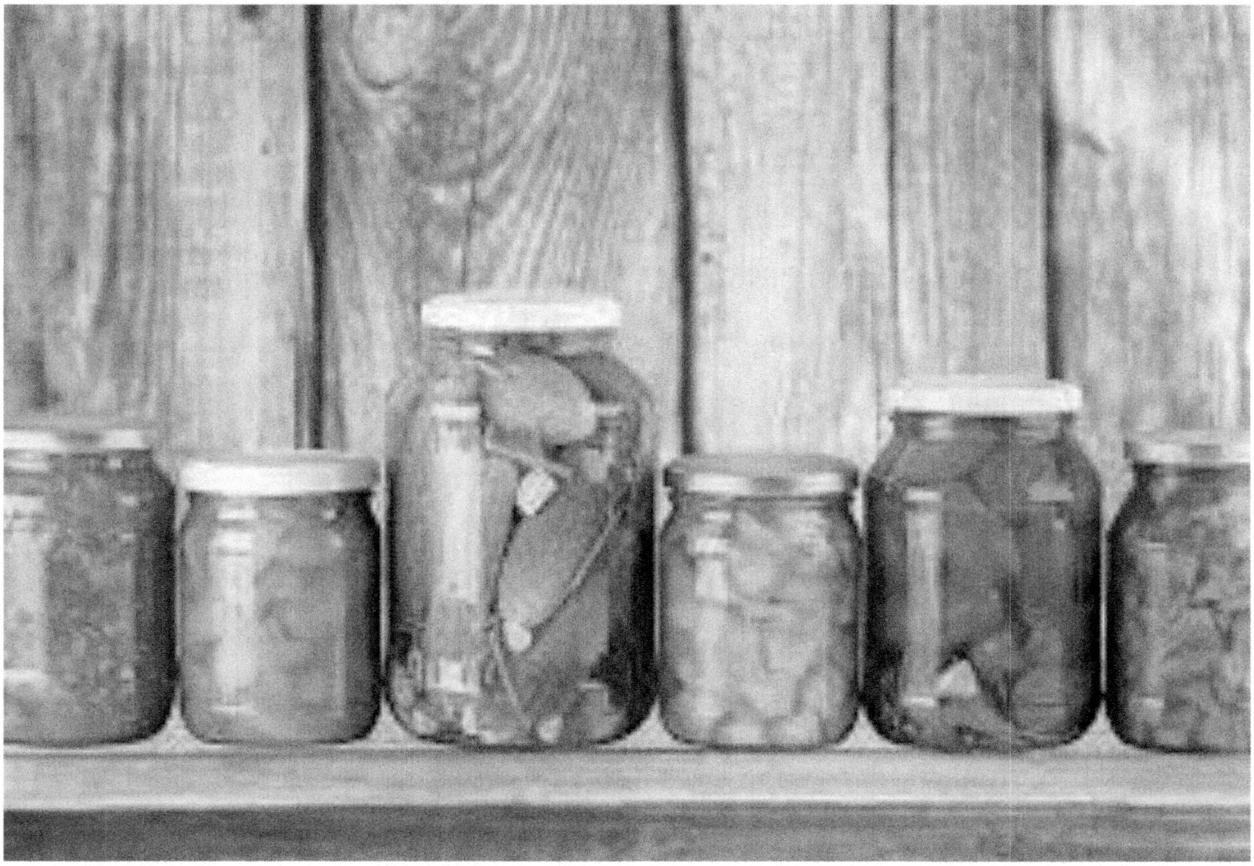

Table of Contents

The Truth About Home Canning 5

Ultimate Home Canning Guide 10

Home Canning For Beginners 13

Home Canning Tomatoes 33

Home Canning Tips 36

Home Canning Equipment 48

The Right Use Of Jars And Lids In Home Canning 57

Get High Quality Food With Home Canning Along With Great Value 61

Home Canning - The Freezing Method 64

Home Canning Preserves Taste and Nutritional Value 66

Home Canning Instructions 69

Home Canning Troubleshooting 73

Canning Botulism 80

The Importance of Using Canning Labels 86

Water Bath Canning Vs. Pressure Canning 90

Pressure Canning Means Food Dyes and Food Coloring Are Out of Your Life 99

Save Money by Canning Food at Home 102

Uses For Used Canning Lids 106

Canning Chicken Breast 111

The Truth About Home Canning

If this year you thought you had your own can, but it's a bit intimidating, don't despair! Learn the difference between truth and myth when it comes to canning at home before you throw your hands away and leave.

Myth one: Canning is too expensive.

True: Canning will save you money!

Most of the cans you need are probably already in your kitchen. Additional basic equipment can be purchased for several dollars. You don't even need a special jar room. You can use a large favorite dish that you already own. You can collect canned goods at the site sale and the savings bank to save money, and once you have, you can re-use for years. The only major costs are, if you want to get into pressure canning food, that you can find for less than $ 100, but that is not necessary for many types of canned food.

After assembling the device, canning can save money. How? Because you can make your own fresh, organic foods for less than you can buy them. Not only that, it's a simple and inexpensive gourmet dish. That pickled asparagus you love so much, and you pay $ 6 for a drink? You can have it for $ 1.50!

Myth two: Canning takes too long.

True: home canning does not take much time than normal cooking.

Of course, you need to cut and prepare fruits and vegetables, and it can look like a lot of time, because you are making a pile at once. But when you think about it, you can do all the preparatory work for one day or to stretch after a whole year, and you end up with the same amount of time spent. The only time that is processing jar, but I think it will save you time when you do not have to go to the store for food! At the end of the day, when you consider everything, it will come out quite evenly.

Myth three: home canning is dangerous.

True: homemade canned food is as safe as other foods.

The instructions and recipes of Canning have been tested and adjusted for the safety of important people who feed on them. They are paid to ensure that the established guidelines protect us all. If you follow these basic instructions, you will be fine.

Myth number four: the food I can use goes wrong.

True: homemade canned food lasts until canned.

In general, the instructions for canned food at home say that food should be consumed within a year. So think about the future. For example, how many glasses of cucumbers did your family eat in a year? Maybe a lot of glasses (or more, because I bet that will increase their consumption when they have a taste of how good home is).

Imagine opening your own homemade fruits and vegetables all year round, and you will not have to rely on factory canned food! I think you'll like it.

Myth five: you have to be a good cook to prove it.

True: if you can read and follow the instructions, Canning is easy.

Canning is really part of cooking, part of Science and part of adventure. When you think about it, it doesn't have to be that intimidating. Entertainment. The directions of Canning are very clear and detailed. There is no need to be a great cook and follow the instructions and finally with some great canned tastings.

Myth six: it is difficult to store homemade canned food.

Truth: no more than any other food you store.

It is a good idea to store canned food in a cool and dark place. And sometimes people complain that they have nowhere to store. Be creative! Do you have an unused shelf in your closet? Do you have a room under your bed? Can you put the shelves in the garage? I think there's room if you think about it.

Myth seven: no one is bored anymore.

True: returns Canning.

With the beginning of all the negative publicity in how our food is raised and brought to us, that people are looking for ways to ensure that we eat healthy and toxic foods. One way to do this is to grow (or buy in farmers ' markets) and own food. It's actually very fashionable!

The truth is that canning is an effective, affordable and easy solution for people who want to be more involved and have more control over your food. If you're a little nervous about starting on your own, find someone to make you a can to help you get past the first batch. You get to the bottom of it, and it turns out all those things you thought were actually myths!

Ultimate Home Canning Guide

Home canning guides are information about how you can and protect your food in the right way. The procedure for preserving food is unequivocally explained. Home canning guides you on every step you take, in terms of food storage and preservation, and how this will result in a good canned product. Canning The Wizard is never complicated, you can do it after understanding its rules. You will be interested in Canning and storing food as you can not imagine.

In the home canning guide, it is better that you need to know all the information. There is a lot to consider before continuing boxing. Know the acidity levels of the food to know which method in Canning you will do. He also knew all the necessary equipment and the basic equipment is a step guide, such as mason jars, lids and two-piece band, large covered water bath or pressure cooker, jar lifter, wide mouth funnel and a rubber spatula. Containers in the canning process, such as water bath containers and pressure vessels. It's like getting back to basics.

Now that you know all the basic things in the Canning family, follow the instructions step by step. Always keep in mind " do "and not " canning guide". Make sure all procedures are correct in Canning and canning.

Abbreviations are not allowed, because they are dangerous and can be harmful. Not following the guide will prove to be a disaster in your conservation and conservation process.

Do not waste time, money and effort by not following certain rules in the Wizard.

This will lead you to all the things you want to know about homemade canned food. It takes you from scratch to an excellent home reservation. Self-discipline is necessary for successful Canning.

Applying all the right procedures, tips and rules in a Can will make you a good guardian. You can leave the food at any time without problems. Thanks to these guides, you will succeed in every canning process, so don't worry about the home canning guide is here.

Home Canning For Beginners

Are you the kind of person who likes to do things the old-fashioned way? I mean keep the traditions and know how things were done before we go through these steps. So let me introduce you to the Canning for beginners. This is one of the best hobbies that anyone can do. You can learn from your grandparents preserved food for the winter. All you need to have is a pressure cooker, some W jars/ lids, some foods you want to try to store and the desire to do so. Pressure cooking traps steam from boiling water to reach the temperature necessary to kill bacteria and make food storage possible.

For beginners, it is better to start with a method of storing boiling water. This is the cheapest way to learn more, and you will be proud of your efforts after it's over. You will need a few jars and lids, both pints and quarters, which are very good for canning tomatoes, pickles and other fruits. Small 8oz jars are good for storing things like taste and jellies. They come 12 in a box and have lids for each. These jars are soaked for canning, and therefore it is not wise to use a jar, such as a jar of mayonnaise or a jar that previously had jelly or jam.

You will also need a very large pan with a lid that is deep enough to cover the cans by at least an inch, and two inches would be even better. You should also have a rack to place the pots to keep them off the bottom. If you do not get a rack with the dish, you can simply place a rack on the bottom of the dish to keep the pots from touching the bottom. Another tool that you will need is a plastic knife or spatula to mix the filled jars and release the trapped air. And a large plastic funnel mouth, and a set of strong, long-handled pot extractors to take the hot pots out of the water. You will need a towel to dry the water from the jars as you remove them from the pan.

Always use the freshest fruits possible and wash and peel the fruits before starting the cooking process. There is a product called fresh fruit that is recommended to prevent the fruit from fading. Read the instructions for getting the recipe for a light, medium or heavy sweet water syrup, experiment to see which one you prefer. Pour this syrup on the fruits. While you are preparing food for cooking, you should put a few jars in the water and let it boil for a few minutes. Then place the food in the hot jars filling about ½ inch from the top. Run the wooden spoon or spatula through the food jars by releasing trapped air. Remove any other food from the outside of the jars, put on the lids and tighten them. Put the jars in the pan and fill them with hot or hot water and put them on the stove. Be sure to cover the jars about an inch above the lid.

Once they have come to a boil, put the lid on the jar. After the water has been boiled vigorously for a few minutes, remove the lid from the jar and let it continue to boil for the time limit in your recipe, usually 10 minutes are good for pickles, and 25 to 30 minutes for fruits, and 35 to 40 minutes for tomatoes.

When you are prepared for the allotted time, turn off the jar and place the jars on a towel to drain and cool, preferably at night. Before letting the pots cool down, check each pot to make sure there are no lids in the middle. If this happens, the food jars are not good because they have not sealed. These can be refrigerated and used immediately so as not to waste fruit. Or they can be annealed to try again, but first use a different lid and dry the lip of the jar before tightening new lids.

There is no better feeling than the feeling you get once you learn to store food. It is useful for those who love to learn how things were done by our grandparents, it is a way of working in the past.

Canning Tips for Beginners

It took me years to try canning at home. Now that I've done it for the last six years, I wish it hadn't taken that long to get started. It's very rewarding because the food you make will be much tastier than anything else on a supermarket shelf.

Tip # 1

Do not put too much pressure on yourself at first. Start with small projects for the foods you like. I recommend jam because the recipes are simple.

Tip # 2

Always use new jar lids. New lids are essential for good sealing. If you start with a new package of pots, then the lids are also new. But if you use old jars, buy new lids. They come in small packages to the place where the pots are sold.

Tip # 3

Fill your bath can with water and start heating it while you assemble the ingredients for your recipe. Once the water will boil and at least 180 to 190 degrees Fahrenheit, use a pot lifter to immerse the pots. Throw the lids in the next one. Hold the water just below the boil and let the objects sterilize for a few minutes. Then take out the jars and lids and place them on a clean countertop or table. Fill them with prepared food.

Tip # 4

Always clean the edges of the jar's mouth thoroughly before applying the lid. The food particles on the mouth of the jar may interfere with sealing.

Tip # 5

Your recipe will refer to the head space in the jar. This is the distance between the top of the food, and the edge of the mouth of the pot. Recipes usually require 1/4" , 1/2 " or sometimes 1 inch of head space. Follow what the recipe says for space, then place the lids on the jars and fix with strips.

Tip # 6

Make sure that a grid is at the bottom of the water bath canning so that the pots do not touch the bottom.

Tip # 7

Be sure to immerse the 1-or 2-inch pots in the boiling water bath. It is important that boiling water completely surrounds the vessels so that heat penetrates from all angles. This is important for the safe preservation of food, as it ensures the destruction of all spores and microbes in food.

Tip # 8

Cover the water bath and let it boil for the time indicated by the recipe. This is often called treatment time.

Tip # 9

After boiling, turn off the fire and remove the lid. Allow the pots to stay in hot water for 5 minutes, then use the pallet jar to remove them.

Tip # 10

Allow the jars to cool undisturbed for 12-24 hours after removing them from the can in a water bath. You will probably hear the eyelids burst in the first few minutes.

Best wishes on your home canning efforts. I consider it a wonderful skill and always encourage others to learn it. Canning is an important part of life autonomy.

Do and what not to do for home Canning

I'm sure more people get better, start storing food. He has a good reason. Canning your own food is a great way to save money. In these difficult economic times, you do not try to do it.

Many beginners need to know that there are certain stages and what not to do for home canning, which are necessary for safe storage of food.

Keep in mind that here is a list of the most common things to consider when storing and storing food at home.

Do

Start with quality fresh fruits and vegetables, which have been thoroughly rinsed and washed with a vegetable brush to remove debris

Use only household glass jars (mason / Kerr jars) with lids and sealing strips in 2 parts

Prepare lids and jars of according to the advice of manufacturers

Choose the appropriate storage method for stored foods

Have all your canning tools handy and ready to use before you start storing your food

Be sure to check your jars for chips or cracks, as this can affect the fact that the jars seal properly and add the risk of breakage during the canning process

Wash and sterilize jars

When filling the tanks, leave enough space on the head

Exactly follow the recipes preservatives

Meet recommended processing times for each Canning project

Store canned food in a cool, dry, dark place

Not to Do

Do not forget to wash your hands before starting the conservation project. Wash again during canning action if you sneeze or need to use the bath

Do not use "commercial" jars, such as spaghetti or mayonnaise. They are not designed for canning and present a high risk of breakage during canning

To seal the jars, use only a strip of 2 pieces and a set of lids. The strips can be used again and again until they are rusty or bent. You can never reuse the lid; Once Upon a time, you will not be able to close it during processing

Do not use an open kettle or any type of oven for storage and canning. The website of the USDA and other authorities indicates that this is no longer a safe way for food

Don't overdo it.

Do not deviate from conservation recipes; it is measured to ensure that food remains safe and is treated properly

The hot liquid in the cold jars does not mix; make sure the jars are heated before filling to avoid breakage

Do not forget to mark canned food with the content and date of treatment

Do not store inverted containers during processing

Unprocessed canned food

Do not remove the lid from the canning jar during processing

Do not try to eat canned foods, which do not seem to be closed properly and have mold or discoloration

The Bottom Line On Home Canning

The final sum on domestic Canning is in case of doubt ask for help. Use common sense when you can and save your food. You want your family to eat healthy and tasteful foods from your canning projects. Give them that chance by following and it's not for canning at home. For your successful home experience.

Canning Provides 3 Things to Do and Don't Do When Canning at Home

If you are new to home canning this year, like so many other people, you will want to follow these simple things to do and not do.

Do

1. Always use new jars and lids-it is important to use jars specially designed for canning. Also, be sure to use brand new caps. You can reuse cans and canning strips from year to year, but always use new lids to ensure good sealing.

2. Always check jars for cracks and chipping-before using a canning jar, be sure to inspect it for cracks or chipping. Look at the edge of the plate. If there is a chip on the rim, you will not get a suitable gasket after processing the plate.

3. Always label preserves-after the preserves have cooled down and are ready to be stored, be sure to label each jar. Write the contents and date canned on the lid with a permanent marker or on a canning label.

Do not do

1. Never pour the hot liquid into a cold jar : you will need to heat your jars before pouring the hot contents into the jar. If you do not, there is a good chance that you will break the pot.

2. Never adjust the recipe-following your recipe when Canning is critical to getting the best results. The use of the right amount of sugar in a jam or jelly recipe is very important. And always treat the jars the right amount of time to give you a safe finished product. Be sure to adjust the processing time according to your altitude.

3. Never tighten the strips too much - when screwing the strips before treatment, make sure not to tighten them too much. You want to adjust them only so that they are tightened to your finger. A good way to make sure you do not over tighten the strips is to screw them using only your thumb and finger.

So, as you can see, if you follow these tips, you will have a successful canning season.

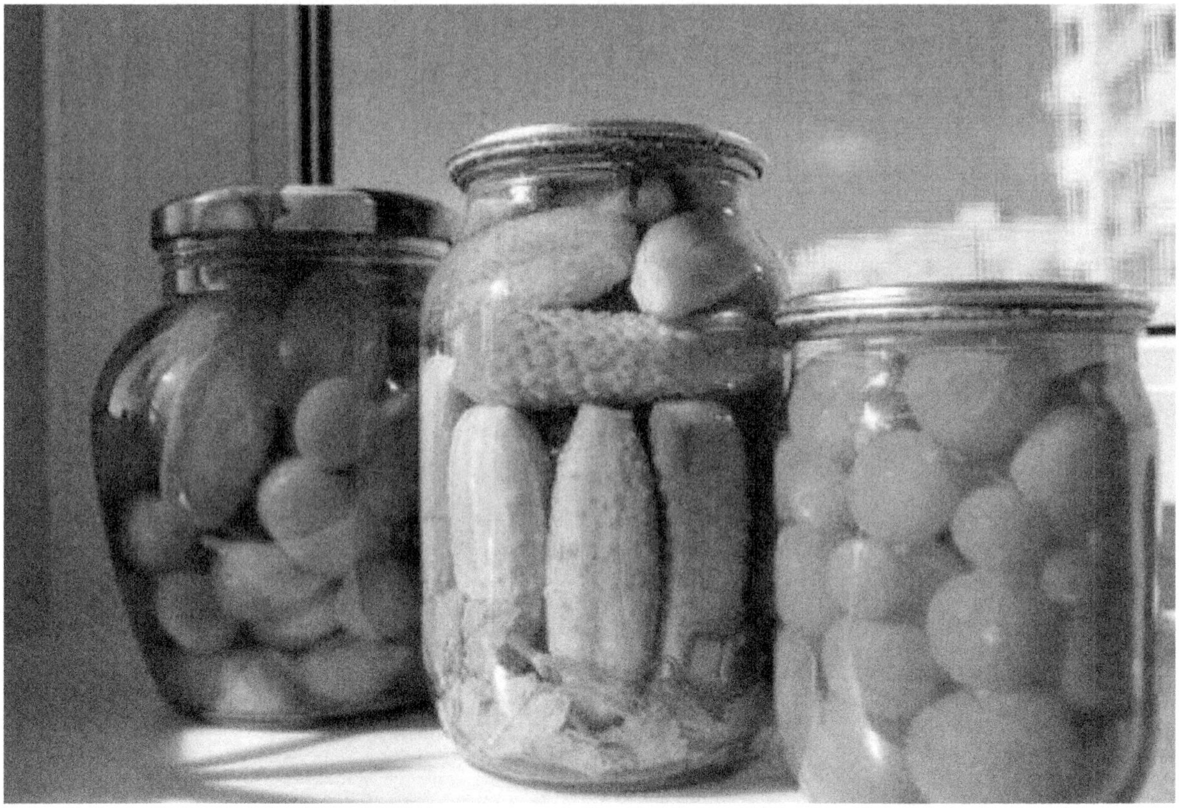

Home Canning Tomatoes

Tomatoes are probably the most popular food grown in gardens.

Usually there is an abundance of this plant once they begin to ripen. Canning tomatoes at home is a way to ensure that the overstock of products is not wasted.

By storing your tomatoes, you can also enjoy the tasty taste of your homemade tomatoes long after the end of the season.

Ways to store tomatoes

There is an assortment of ways to store tomatoes. They can be canned, frozen or in some cases even dried. The most popular way of storing Tomatoes is canning.

This versatile method allows you to use canned tomatoes in a variety of techniques that can be used later to prepare soups, chili or stews.

Who would not want the same great taste of fresh tasting, even in the cold winter months?

Preparation of canned tomatoes

When preparing tomatoes for canning, you need to use only a stainless steel pot or frying pan and stainless steel utensils.

Since tomatoes have such a high acid value, the use of any other type of jar can cause bitter-flavored canned tomatoes that have a less than desirable color on them.

Canned Tomatoes Safely

It is important to remember that to ensure the safety of tomatoes must be stored properly. Choose only fresh and disease-free tomatoes for canning. Tomatoes tend to be acidic foods. Methods of Canning in a boiling water bath or canning under pressure are the recommended processing technique for canning tomatoes at home. According to some sources, the use of a pressure preservative can also give a better quality flavor with a more nutritious value. Or, Nevertheless, it is an acceptable way of storing tomatoes.

The USDA recommends that all canned tomatoes at home be acidified before canning to ensure safety against botulism. This is achieved by adding 2 tablespoons of lemon juice or 1/2 teaspoon of citric acid per liter. Using pints, add 1 tablespoon of lemon juice or 1/4 teaspoon of citric acid.

The processing time of hot-packed crushed tomatoes in a can in a water bath is 35 minutes for pints and 45 minutes for pints. If you use a pressure preservative, then the treatment time is 15 minutes for pints and pints. You need to be sure to set the dial gauges on the 11-pound pressure cooker. the pressure and weighted gauge should be set to 10 pounds. pressure.

Home Canning Tips

Home canning can be one of the most rewarding projects you can do for your family. Knowing that the food you cook with is fresh and has not been filled with additives or preservatives can be very comforting and satisfying. With so many positive aspects of this process that our grandmother has always done, why has it become a lost art in many homes? Simple, people tend to stay away from things they don't know how to do. Home canning is a process that is not difficult even for beginners to learn and can save money in the long run, and with a few tips, Who knows, you could even become an expert.

There are many different recipes of jellies, jams, preserves, whole fruits, vegetables, and much more that you can preserve through home canning, and you can usually find many of them are friends and family or online. The focus of our home canning tips will be on the canning process itself and some of the issues you may encounter. The three areas we will talk about are: adjustment, sealing and storage. Many people are frustrated by these areas in one way or another, but I have some tips that you might find useful and could change your attitude towards home canning.

Setting

How many of you were so happy to make your own strawberry jam only to be disappointed to find out that you made strawberry syrup instead? Learning how to tell whether jelly or jam will be set can be difficult at first, but hopefully with a few tips you will get the hang of it. Or if the jam or jelly goes can be subordinated to a number of factors.

We'll talk about pectin, baby.:

There are several things you will need to consider every time you add pectin to your jam or jelly, the first is, although you do not add it. There are a few recipes out there that you can use that don't add pectin if you want to follow this path, but as we'll talk about later, the relationship is important. So do not take a recipe that has the indications for adding pectin and decide that you will try to make it work without pectin, as it will not work. If you are using pectin, you should make sure that the pectin you are using is recent and has not been sitting on a shelf for a long time. Pectin can and will expire and this will affect the process of gelling jelly or jam. I always wait until I decide to make a jam or jelly before going to buy my pectin.

Many different fruits have different amounts of pectin, so for example, usually I don't have to use the whole bag of pectin when I make blackberry jam, but when I make strawberry jam, I definitely have to use the whole bag. Usually the fruits will have enough pectin to help you in the adjustment process. The frustrating task is to work with certain vegetables or peppers and set them up because they naturally have less pectin in them. A good rule of thumb is to look online for how much pectin could be in the selected fruit or vegetable before you start making jelly. For example, blackberry jam= 1/2 bag of pectin, strawberry jam = one bag of pectin, chili jelly = 2 bags of pectin.

As if this is not enough to consider, we throw another monkey into the key and look at the dry pectin in relation to the liquid pectin. In my experience, I had to use two sachets of liquid pectin to achieve the same results as a leakproof bag. I'm sure it probably varies from person to person. In addition, there are several recipes for liquid pectin and dry pectin that you put them in the recipe at different times.

Liquid pectin will usually enter after Sugar has been inserted while dry pectin will be inserted before sugar. I know I know, you're probably ready to go to the store, instead and just buy jelly from the shelf. The trick is to find a process that works for you, and stay with it.

I suggest you find the process that works best for you and stay with it for a while, so you can really understand what you're doing every time you decide to try and let it go.

One last thing about pectin before you leave. There are certain types of pectin products that you can use that do not require you to add sugar like, Pomona. Again, there are specific recipes that you'll need to look at to get the right ratios, but these are usually very useful for diabetics out there who would like can have their own jelly or jam without all the added sugar.

Ripe or not ripe...that's the Question

As my grandmother used to say, " somewhere in the middle is good."The trick is to know where the center really is. If you get your fruits before they are ripe, it does not fix them, if you get your fruits at the end of the season, most likely, it will not take. It is difficult to work with, but knowing the age of the fruits and vegetables you work with is very important. That's why working with products that were purchased at the grocery store can be very frustrating. If you do not have your own garden, fruit trees, I suggest you go to a producer market or an orchard where you know where your food comes from. I'm not saying that because of biological fear or pesticides or hormonal fears blah blah blah. It's just overall less frustrating in the end.

And finally, if you still have problems with setting jam or jelly, you may need to look at the ratio of the ingredients you use in your recipe. Compare with other recipes you may encounter. Try different recipes. When I made my first batch of jelly, I became so consumed by following the recipe to the letter that I ignored the process. I followed the indications, boil, add pectin, stir for a minute, add sugar, mix, boil for a minute, put in jars. I did perfectly, but guess what. He wasn't ready. Some tips you can use during this process: use a stainless steel perforated ladle and test the jelly on a cold plate. Stop worrying about 1 minute here 2 minutes here and notice the process. Before I even put my fruit in the oven, I'll put a plate in the freezer. When I add pectin, I make sure that all the pectin has melted and none of them have crumpled. Then, while I stir after adding the sugar, I will take the cold plate from the freezer and once all the sugar is dissolved, I will put a small sample on the plate and set it aside, then continue stirring on low heat. After a minute, I will run my finger to the center of the sample of jelly or jam that I put on the plate and there should be a clear mark in the center of the dish without jam or jelly. If the jelly comes back inside, I know that I need to add more pectin or cook for a little more. Some will add more sugar, but I find that jelly / jam usually already has a lot of sugar and that adding more it will usually make it too sweet.

Sealing

So finally made the recipe, and you can tell your jelly or jam will set correctly and now you want to make sure it seals. One of the biggest mistakes that is most often made by many people, myself included, is the reuse of lids. I know it can be very tempting, and I understand that it is very difficult to throw away the other lids and buy new ones, but believe me...it's just that it's better this way.

Reuse lids = not a good idea

In the end, it usually ends just in frustration. A good advice for home canning, if it could lead to frustration later, do not. Markets will sell the lids separately so you can reuse the jars and rings, but the lids must be a reinvestment that you plan to do each year. Another mistake that is often made is the idea that you can reuse the jars of food you bought at the grocery store.

You can make a small investment in mason jars that you can permanently reuse each year and store easily. If you reuse the jars of food, you will not be able to close the lids, and the integrity of the glass was not made for continuous heating and heating necessary to properly process the jars.

Store

This might not seem like a very important topic when it comes to home canning tips, but I believe these may be the most important tips in this entire article. Many people have different systems or shelves or pantry that they use to store their canned products at home and you can get a lot of these ideas online. There are important things to remember whenever you are looking for a place to store your canned products at home.

A great tip for storing your canned items at home is to label them, what they are, the date they were processed, etc. Also, Be sure to store the old items in the front to make sure you eat them first. Temperature is also a very important consideration in your choice of storage. It is important to store your items in a place that can maintain a temperature between 50-70 degrees Fahrenheit. Some people like to freeze their food. If you want to do this, I suggest you look at some of the freezable plastic containers that can be used to safely store food in the freezer. Do not use glass jars to store in the freezer, as it could lead to breaking them to begin with. I can also break the seal you had on the lid causing the food to become burnt or at best pasty freezer. You also want to make sure that the area you choose is out of sunlight and not close to moisture. High temperatures can cause food to spoil, and sunlight can cause food to lose nutrition, so it is best to keep them in a dry and dark place. For these reasons, many people choose to store them in a basement, but make sure that they are not exposed to moisture because moisture can cause corrosion of the lids and eventually thaw.

Home Canning Equipment

Public protest food practices in our country stimulates a renewed interest in Canning domestique...et for good reason!

Canning food at home ensures that nothing toxic gets into the food you and your family consume. And it also tastes better! It is a winner / winner in my books.

Do not let the idea of Canning intimidate you. It is not as difficult as you might think.

Also, you will not have to invest your life savings to start a home canning operation in your home.

In fact, most of the equipment you need probably already owner.

Here is a list of essentials and other things you might want to collect over time:

Mason Jars

Often you can find these glass jars in cheap garage sales. Swipe your finger around the edge of the jar (when buying used) to make sure you don't feel chipping or bumps. Even the slightest chip will prevent the ships from sealing. Most grocery stores sell pots of different sizes from case to case during the summer and autumn Canning seasons. (Note: do not use recycled mayonnaise and other seasoning jars for canning-only use mason jars created for canning purposes.)

Seal the jar lids can

While you can buy pots and reuse them again and again, the lids of the pots should be new. These small metal lids have a horrible strip around them that once hot, create the seal between the lid and the jar. If you buy new jars by chance, these lids will be included. If you reuse old jars, then the lids can be purchased separately and are inexpensive.

Bands or rings of vase

These metal rings screw the jar to create a snug fit between the jar and the lid. They can be reused, and you do not need to buy new ones every time. If you find your short term on the rings, you can remove them from completely fresh jars that have already been canned and sealed. It is not necessary to store them with screwed strips. Again, if you buy new vases by Chance, The Rings will be included in the package, but you can buy them separately.

Canned Boiling Water

It's not as intimidating as it sounds…you can use a large pot or another large pot of deep sauce that you already own. I keep my jams and jellies for years before investing in a pot of water (which I found at a garage sale for $5!) The vase you use should be large enough that the vessels that store are completely submerged with about 2 inches or more of water above the jars) and with enough space around the pots so that the water can move freely).

If you are using a pot from your kitchen, you must have a good sized lid to go with it. You will also need to buy a metal stand (you can buy them separately in the same section of the pots in most stores) or make a home-made solution so that your pots do not sit on the bottom of the pot without protection.

A great homemade solution I used was to put as many pot rings side by side on the bottom of the pan as it would fit. The pots then sat on the rings, creating a gap between the pot and the bottom of the pot.

Kitchen Utensils

Things like measuring spoons, wooden spoons (long-handled ones work best), ladles, funnels, spatulas, etc.

Not essential (but very useful additions):

Pole-And-Line Ship

This simple clamp gadget is specially designed to safely lift boiling water bath pots when the pots are too hot to touch.

Although it is not essential, it is difficult to do without it (I have already used ordinary kitchen tongs, which is difficult.

Wet jars tend to want to get out of the socket and dropping a glass jar full of hot and hot food is something you absolutely want to avoid!)

Lever Cover

This is a small plastic stick with a magnet on the bottom to make it easier to lift the jar lids from the hot water in which you sat them while storing them.

This small pusher is absolutely not essential, but very economical and quite smooth.

I haven't had one in years, but after taking it, I wondered why I hadn't released the $ 2 a long time ago. I love it!

Bubble Remover and headspace tool

If you want to be sure of the head space you leave, there is no better way to measure it with a device specially designed to complete the work. Some people swear by them, but it was never something I used.

Pressure Gun

This is the most expensive investment of the entire canning process, but you can take one for less than $75.00 and it will last forever, at least! (I bequeathed my grandmother).

Even though I didn't put it in the MUST HAVE section, it's a must if you're going to box low-acid stuff like most vegetables, meats, etc.However, there are many, many recipes that you may not need a pressure preservative, so it's not essential for all preserves. My suggestion is that if you are new to Canning, try your hand at the water bath method of Canning before dipping into recipes that require pressure canning.

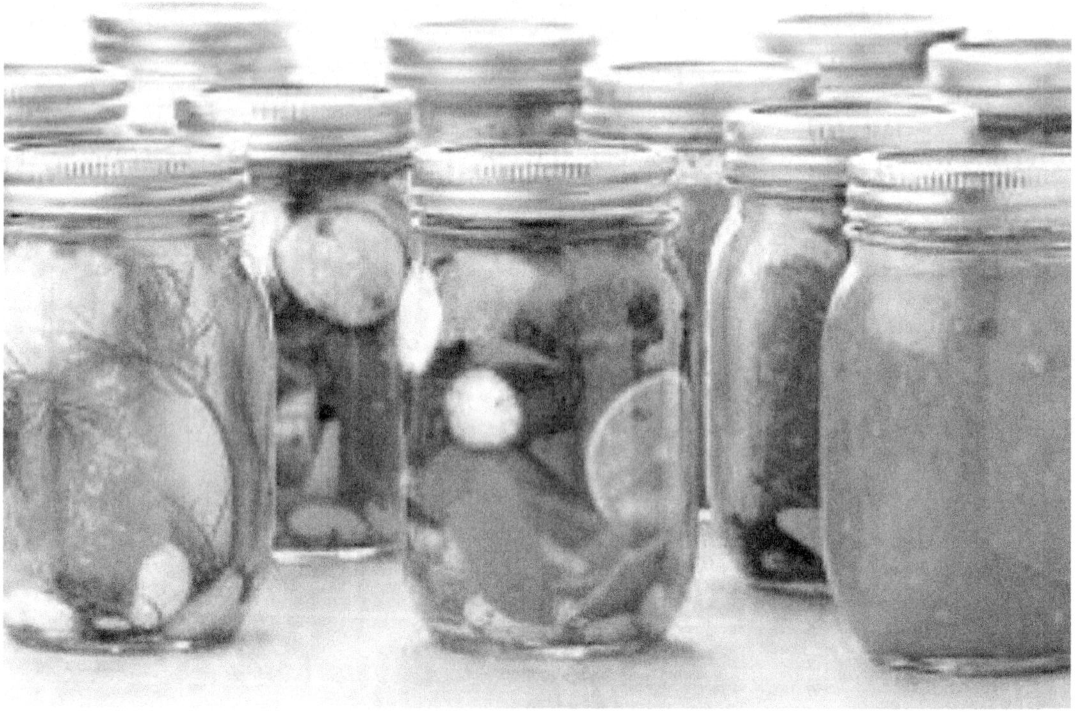

The Right Use Of Jars And Lids In Home Canning

Glass jars are undoubtedly the best way to proceed in home canning, whether it is canning under pressure or canning in a boiling water bath. I would never use metal containers because of the one-time use and, most importantly, the requirement and cost of sealing equipment in the use of metal cans.

Jar with its regular, wide open mouth threaded neck for sealing ring and lids are definitely the best for home canning. Your mason jar requires only lids every time it is used at home canning. It is necessary to wash the jars before each use in warm water. The use of a mild detergent is necessary with rinsing after cleaning. This will not sterilize the vessels, but cleans the vessels for prolonged boiling of water or canning under pressure.

However, if you plan to prepare jams, jellies or pickled items, this requires sterilization of the vessels in the home canning procedure. This is a simple and easily achievable procedure by placing empty pots in a barrel of boiling water. Fill the pots and hot pot, but not boiling water, an inch above the mouth of the pot. This should be boiled for ten minutes at altitudes below 1000 feet and add an extra minute for each 1000 foot altitude change. I will provide a reference at the end where you can find a graph on this complete procedure.

The jar requires a good lid and seal. In food processing, the lid seal seals the sealing surface of the jar, but leaves enough space to allow air to escape from the jar, which allows the seal to form an airtight seal on the domestic canning jar. I would buy only the number of lids you will need in your home canning efforts for a season. This way you can be sure that you have fresh lids and seals.

Now you have your jars full and to release the air bubbles using a flat plastic spatula, no metal please insert between the food and the edge of the jar. Slowly moving the jar in a circle, push the spatula up and down to encourage air release and leakage bubbles.It is necessary to clean the edge of the pot by removing particles that would prevent an airtight seal.

Now you are ready for action! Proceed to place the lid seal on the clean edge of the pot and mount the flat metal lid into the metal screw ring and slowly turn down on the seal being careful not to over tighten the lid in this procedure. It's time to process the filled jars and when this is done, carefully remove the domestic canning jars with a jar handle cleaner.

It will not be necessary to tighten the lids again. The cooling of the vessels causes the contents of the vessel to contract which in turn firmly pulls the self-sealing lid to the mouth of the vessel resulting in a high vacuum. Pots should be cooled for twelve or twenty-four hours at room temperature in an upright position.

Then it's time to remove the screw rings from the jars and start testing each lid for the correct seal. This is done easily by pressing the center of the lid to see if it is concave. Then lift the jar from its lid to see if it will come off and if you can't achieve it and the center doesn't want to flex up or down, you have a good seal and your home canning is over.

Get High Quality Food With Home Canning Along With Great Value

To be honest, Home Canning is a lot of work. I like to say that it's a wonderful pastime if you want to stand in a kettle of boiling water in July. So why are I and so many other slave people away from storing food at home?

In defense of home canning, it is not so unusual for someone to work hard on a hobby that he likes, and home canning is a very satisfying activity. Consuming foods that have been stored at home provides a pleasant feeling of accomplishment and independence, besides the food tastes good.

Your home canning efforts will also allow you to source the highest quality food and taste. You can avoid wasting abundant crops from your garden or a good deal in an agricultural market. Properly preserved fresh fruits, taste, jams, jellies, soups, vegetables, sauces and so on taste much better than most mass-produced alternatives from the supermarket. This superior quality compensates for your work because you get good food that money cannot buy because you have to do it yourself. In addition, when you can eat for yourself and your family, you can select food at the peak of freshness and treat it. This compares quite favorably to store-bought foods bouncing around a truck on the way to a processing plant. When you select your food, you are the judge of quality. You can also pursue organic products when available. And buying a local producer allows you to support the local economy. Of course, the most satisfying way of food is to grow products yourself.

The high quality of canned food at home makes it a good value, although the investments of effort and equipment for home canning make the food at the same price as the supermarket food. Good food creates a better quality of life. You will get used to canned food so much that when you are finished and have to buy something in the store, you will invariably be disappointed.

In addition to good taste, there is another important reason to incorporate home canning into your dietary nutrition as much as possible. Commercial canned products are coated with an epoxy resin that most often contains a chemical called bisphenol - A (BPA). You may have heard as a toxic ingredient in plastic bottles, such as water bottles and baby bottles. Eating canned food commercially often exposes you to BPA, which is a hormone that disrupts the chemistry associated with neurotoxicity and cancer. By storing your food in glass cans, you will avoid BPA. Eating fresh or frozen foods is also a way to avoid canned products exposed to BPA.

With practice and good recipes, you can enjoy tasty foods and avoid exposure to a harmful chemical. After completing a few successful home-made canned projects, you will taste the difference and probably not be ashamed to even brag about your achievements.

Home Canning - The Freezing Method

You probably know that many people jumped on the wagon when it comes to preserving their food. What if I told you that even if you've never tried Canning alone, is there an approach that anyone can learn easily? Home preserves-the freezing process is the best way to start.

Although there are many ways to store and store food available to try the freezing method is a favorite among Canning enthusiasts for a number of reasons:

The freezing approach takes less time than other home canning methods.

Learning the process of freezing fresh fruits and vegetables is easy and accessible even for beginners.

Generally, the cost involved in freezing your food is minimal.

Frozen Fruits and vegetables can be stored for a year without affecting the taste and quality of food.

You have the will to prepare meals quickly by simply opening the freezer.

Almost all vegetables require sunburn before freezing. Bleaching is a step in the process of preparing food for freezing. This is not difficult to learn, but there are defined processing times for vegetables to blanch based on which ones you want to freeze. There are some exceptions to this rule, such as onions and fresh green peppers that do not require sunburn to store them in the freezer.

Fruits are another source that does not need to be blanched before freezing. Typically, the fruits should be peeled (animated even if necessary) and have a preservative applied to them such as fresh fruit or lemon juice to discourage any discoloration and to block the fresh taste of the fruit that will freeze.

Now you know that the House preserves - the method of freezing is an easy way even for a beginner to get started. There are steps to this process, but they are not difficult to learn. You can also do it.

Home Canning Preserves Taste and Nutritional Value

For a long time, home canning has occupied an important place in the preservation of local fruits and vegetables. It has many advantages. Commercially preserved foods use chemicals and pesticides in large quantities while foods stored at home are not highly exposed to chemicals and pesticides. In addition, commercially prepared spreads and sauces contain added amounts of sugar, salts and preservatives that are not necessary for a good healthy diet. In fact, it can cause harm to people suffering from diabetes or hypertension.

Home Canning Provides Better Nutrition

Preservation of food at full ripeness will allow home preservatives to taste spreadable creams and flavored sauces throughout the year.

According to Jennifer Wilkins, a nutrition scientist at the Department of Life Sciences at Cornell University, a completely torn food has a higher nutritional value when stored.

He gives the example of tomatoes in which vitamin C increases when tomatoes are fully ripe in the vine.

Makes You Autonomous

According to master gardener and home conservator Connie Densmore, in the event of a natural disaster when food supplies are short, people will have their own food to eat. In addition, it says that canned food at home can last for years without refrigeration (especially useful if the power goes out) while maintaining the same taste as the day they were collected.

This Is The Best Method For Storing Food

Previously, it was one of the few ways to preserve and save food from microorganisms.

Home canning methods began in the late 1800s to prevent spoilage of food by enzymes, molds, yeasts and bacteria.

Resources That Can Help People Learn More

People who want to store food using this method should refer to the US Department of Agriculture's "complete guide to home canning" which can be found online.

The guide explains the methods of Canning for a variety of foods.

HomeCanning.com it also offers a number of recipes for canning fruits, vegetables and meats. It is Jarden home Brands, site that is one of the leading suppliers of pots and equipment. Other suppliers include pantry canning and supply home and specialty preserves.

Home Canning Instructions

Two main processes are used to Channel Food. We will discuss boiling water bath and steaming Canning in this article.

Both methods will use enough heat to kill organisms that cause food spoilage.

Water Bath Canning

If you are going to canned fruits, pickles or any other food with a high content of acid, this is the method to use. Make sure you canner has a rack and a tight mounting cover.

They should also be deep enough to cover your vessels at least two inches. Make sure that your jars do not have cracks or chips before the canning process.

Canning Steam Pressure

This method should be used when you have low-acid foods such as vegetables, chicken and meat.

To safely process these foods, you need to prepare them at warmer temperatures than boiling water.

Canning

Use only fresh fruits and vegetables. Wash them in water but do not bruise them. Pack the vegetables and fruits in a jar and pour the liquid you intend to use to channel them. Common liquids used for canned food are water, syrup and fruit juice. If you store corn, peas or lima beans, give them space in the pot to allow them to grow.

Hot Water Bath Canning Process

Add the jars in hot or boiling water. Make sure that the water fills about an inch above the pots. Once the water starts to boil, start timing the process. Let it boil for the specified time that it takes to cook the food you have in the jar. Continue to add more water as the initial water begins to boil.

Gun Pressure Instructions

Put two or three inches of boiling water in the pot. For Steam circulation, place the vessels on a grid. Tighten the lid and make sure it is fully connected. Let the steam out regularly for ten minutes, before closing the tap.

Once the pressure rises to ten kilograms, start counting the time for the process. At the end of cooking, remove it from the fire and allow it to cool. Take out the jar and make sure it is sealed. Now you will be able to store canned food.

If you keep at high altitude, increase the processing time by one minute for every 1000 feet above sea level.

Home Canning Troubleshooting

I like homemade preserves. There is a huge satisfaction to see the beautiful preserves lined up on the counter after finishing canning a batch of food. However, all my canning efforts are not successful. Here are seven things that can go wrong when canning and what you can do to help prevent some of these failures.

Food darkens on jars

* The liquid did not cover all the food. Completely cover the food before covering the jars. As long as the vessels have been properly processed the dark color does not imply deterioration.

* Food has not been processed long enough to destroy enzymes. Always treat food according to the recommended methods and during the recommended periods.

* Air was sealed in the containers either because the head space was too large or because the air bubbles were not removed. To remove air bubbles, perform a rubber spatula between the food and the jar before putting on the lid.

Loss of fluid during treatment

* If the food is not heated before packaging, it will lead to loss of liquid during treatment.

* Food packed too tight.

* Air bubbles will not remove before treatment. Run a rubber spatula between the food and the jar to remove air bubbles.

* Pots were not covered with water in a barrel in a boiling water bath. Pots should be covered 1 inch above the tops in the water bath preserves throughout the process.

* During canning under pressure, the temperature was allowed to fluctuate. The temperature during canning of pressure should remain constant.

* Starches absorb liquids; there is nothing you can do to avoid this.

Fruit Of The Fleet

* The fruit is lighter than syrup. Use firm ripe fruits and heat them before wrapping. Use light or medium syrup and pack the fruit as close as possible without crushing it.

Lids With Buckle

* The screw strips were too tight during machining. Be sure to gently screw the lids before treatment.

* Food spoilage can cause gases inside the jar to force the lid to close or unpack. Always treat food according to recommended times and methods to avoid spoilage.

Seal the jars and unpack them

* Deterioration of food can cause this. Do not eat foods that you suspect may be spoiled.

* Food particles left on the sealing surface can cause the vessels to open. Be sure to wipe the circles of the jars with a clean cloth before sealing.

* Cracks in the jars will not allow the jars to remain sealed. Be sure to carefully check all pots before using them.

Green Vegetables Brown

* Vegetables are cooked or overripe for canning.

Lids become rusty or corroded

* Lids may become rusty or corroded if food is not prepared properly. Always follow the recommended guidelines.

* Incorrect head space in the vessels.

* Do not remove the strips before storing the jars closed. When the jars are ready to be stored, remove the strips, then clean and dry them before storing for next use.

The most dangerous thing that can go wrong in Canning is spoilage. Food that is ruined or that you believe may be ruined should never be eaten. Some of the most obvious signs of deterioration include gas bubbles and splashes of liquid, soft, pasty, viscous or musty food, cloudy liquid, leaking pots, protruding lids, and unnatural odors and colors. It's always better to be sure than sorry. Get rid of any food you think you have ruined.

The best way to prevent most of the problems listed above is to make sure you follow all the instructions for processing your food. I also find that if I try to do "too much" at once I am tired and tend to make mistakes that cause my pots to not turn properly. It is better to do only a few batches of food at a time and take a break in between.

Even if you will always have cans that do not turn out correctly, the more you can eat, the less mistakes you will have. So, keep storage and enjoy your great fruits and vegetables all year round.

Canning Botulism

There is a recent increase in interest in home canning. With this interest came a wave of concerns about the safety of home canning.

Most people turn to home canning in order to make healthier choices for themselves and their families. Making them sick is counterproductive!

The truth is that if you are sloppy about what you do and do not follow the rules, you create a wonderful environment for the problems that occur.

However, if you are a conscientious conservative who follows USDA-approved guidelines, your risk of foodborne illness is low or not.

What is botulism?

One of the biggest fears in home canning is botulism. Botulism is caused by a bacterium that is literally everywhere. However, this bacterium is not the problem. This is when the bacterium enters a perfect environment to grow, it creates a toxin. Toxin is what is deadly.

This rare, but often fatal, food-borne disease develops well in low-acid, moist, airless environments. The ideal place to grow a lot of botulism is in a jar of poorly preserved low-acid foods (such as meats or vegetables).

One scary thing about botulism is that you can't say it's there (unless you're in a lab environment and you're looking for it). Infected foods will not be different.

Symptoms of botulism

After consuming something containing botulism, it usually takes 12-38 hours (but sometimes up to 10 days) for the onset of symptoms. It is important to get medical help immediately.

Although only about 20-25 cases of botulism occur per year, about 10% of them are fatal. Treating it early is a key to survival.

Some of the symptoms to watch out for include dry mouth, blurred vision, speech disorders, vomiting, diarrhea, difficulty swallowing, and respiratory failure.

Safe Canning = Healthy Food

The best way to protect yourself and others from canned botulism at home is to follow safe canning practices. Here are some things to keep in mind that you can:

1. Follow all instructions religiously. Do not skimp on processing times. Don't change the recipe unless it says you can.

2. Use only USDA approved recipes. Yes, this means that it is not safe to use your grandmother's recipe, even if it keeps for years and no one has been sick. The canning practices have changed as more information becomes available. Stay safe and use safe recipes.

3. Do not change the acid content of the foods you store. Acid and Heat are the two main defenses against botulism.

4. Use good hygiene in the kitchen. Make sure all your equipment is clean and your jars are properly sterilized.

5. Make sure the jars are sealed after being canned. If not sealed, store in the refrigerator and eat early.

6. Make sure you have your gun pressure checked every year. This is a free service offered in most regions. Check around and see when and where it is offered near you. It is important to know that your gauge and jar seal are working properly.

7. When you open a jar of low-acid foods to eat, boil the contents for 20 minutes to help destroy germs that can hide inside.

Do not let the fear of botulism prevent you from creating your own canning.

Just follow the appropriate procedures and use approved recipes. People have enjoyed the benefits of canned food at home for years.

Do it safely and you can join their ranks!

The Importance of Using Canning Labels

Canning labels are an essential part of the tools of any household preservative. While using labels is a safe way to enhance your home canning experience, there are several ways to label your canned products.

The easiest way to label your canning is to write on the lid of the jar with a sharpie. Some manufacturers produce canning lids that have lines printed on the lid specially for labeling purposes. Although it is a fast and dirty method, it is not very pleasant visually. It also presents a big problem. After consuming the contents of the jar, the lid is always labeled for old food and is difficult to reuse. If you want a cleaner looking more professional, way to label your canning, you can use the stick on the labels.

The sticks on the labels are available in two forms, those made to be attached to the lid of the jar and those intended to be attached to the jar itself. There is a wide variety of two types of labels to use. Buying sticks on labels at the local office supply store is a solution. Unfortunately, these labels are not designed specifically for canning and will not be very durable. Some websites offer specific Canning labels that you can download and print at home. These labels will be designed to contain important storage information, such as date, content and batch number, but should always be printed on weak material. The best solution is to order specific labels for canning online. You will be able to get the widest range of colors and durable designs and labels. These sites have waterproof labels, which is important because canning involves water baths.

Although there is a wide variety of labelling solutions, it is essential that a certain type of labelling be used for a variety of reasons. You need to label the content, the date in the box, the batch number and the name of the conservators.

Labeling the contents of the jar may seem simple, but it is very important. For example, there are many types of jams or pickles, and it can be difficult to identify what kind of blueberry jam is in a jar. In addition, if you plan to give your canning as a gift to family and friends, it will not be so easy for them to identify what is in a particular jar.

Date is one of the most important things to label on canning jars. The date is important because you can remember when you canned a favorite food and you can plan your future Canning projects when the food of your feet is the freshest.

Date labeling also prevents you from eating very old jars that may have been lurking in your pantry for years. It also helps to move the older jars to the front of the pantry so that they are eaten first and prevent spoilage.

Lot number is an easy way to handle deterioration if it occurs. When you can large amounts of food, do several errands in your canning. If a particular pot goes wrong too soon, you can easily identify which batch it was by checking the condition of the other pots in that specific batch.

Canning labels are important tools for home preservatives and should always be used. They will improve the appearance of your pots, help you remember what is in the pots and the date when they were canned.

Water Bath Canning Vs. Pressure Canning

When choosing how to pickle or what pickle recipes you want to try, there are a number of things you want to keep in mind. One of these things is the canning method you want to use. Home canning is a very simple process that can be done in two ways: Canning under pressure or canning in a water bath. Pressure canning is a process that requires pressure canning, which can often be costly at times. You may however be able to find a cheap one with a bit of hunting through garage sales or flea markets. Canning of the water bath, on the other hand, can be done using only a few simple tools. We assume that you use a method of storage in a water bath. The following article will explain this particular method.

First of all, of course, you will need a pot in a water bath. You need to make sure it is deep enough to hold enough water to soak the canning jars at least 1 inch. You will also need your own jars, screw strips and canning lids. It is much cheaper, tried and true means of Canning. It is a way to store hundreds of foods, including sauce, jam, jelly, pickled fruits and vegetables, as well as taste for hundreds of years. This is an excellent canning method for beginners, or avid conservatives.

A water bath preservative is essentially a large pot with a holder that can hold up to seven quart mason jars or up to sixteen pint jars. Using a large stock jar and being creative with yarn, you can improvise a rack to create your own water bath canister. As long as the pots avoid direct heat from the burner and are completely immersed in water, a number of cunning configurations can be used. If you want to save the rigging problem on your own, they can be easily purchased in many places or online.

The way a water bath preservative works is that it increases the temperature of your canning jar to a temperature hot enough to kill the yeast, bacteria and mold that are found in food. The heat also creates air bubbles that push the air inside the jar as the heat contained in the jar and grow. When the pot cools to room temperature, the air pressure creates a seal that prevents air and other organisms from entering the pot, preventing food from deteriorating, hence the reason for the existence of Canning.

It is essential that the pots are free of scratches or cracks and the edge is flat. They also need to be washed recently, by hand or in the dishwasher, so that they are sterile and free of microorganisms. The process begins by filling the tin can with the desired ingredients. Be sure to wipe the edge with a washed towel in order to create an ideal seal. Place the lid on the circle, making sure to center it so that the rubber is all over the circle, and then screw the tape. The group does not need to be screwed firmly; too narrow strips do not allow gases to escape from the vessels. Then you will place the pots in the water bath on the rack. Make sure the water is covering all the pots by at least an inch and then bring the water to a boil. When finished, turn off the fire and let stand for five minutes before removing the jars from the pot. Be sure to let the jars cool down, so as not to get burned.

As the pots cool down, the tops should be closed while sealing, which means that; after sealing the tops will not depress by pressing with your finger. If the jars are not sealed, the center of the lid opens and at the bottom when pressed. Either discard these jars or eat the contents within a week. If the lids do not seal, do not use them again as they do not seal if they are used again.

After the pots have cooled, they can be stored. It is better if they are stored in a cool, dark place such as a cellar or pantry. The contents will be ready to eat according to the recipe. Make sure that before eating, the contents are inspected for signs of deterioration: mold, gas, cloudiness, odors or drainage. If the deterioration has occurred, do not eat the contents of the can as this can cause serious illness.

Here is a simple pickling recipe to try!

Delicious Pickles:

Wash cucumbers, pack in sterilized jars.

Solution (enough for 3 liters of pickles in glass jars):

1 gallon of vinegar

1 cup salt

½ Pound (16 tablespoons) of dry mustard, be sure to mix the dry mustard well with vinegar so that there are no lumps. A good way to do this is to take a little vinegar and make a kind of dough substance with mustard powder, and then mix the vinegar.

Pour the mixture over the cucumbers into the sterilized jars and seal simultaneously (using the method of your choice.). Store the pickles without removing the screw strips.

Discovering the Secrets of Water Bath Canning

Canning in a water bath is the process of canning food in boiling water and processing. Foods with high levels of acid are suitable for this canning process, since most of the bacteria in these foods can only be easily killed by boiling them. The required temperature in this method of Canning is 100 degrees Celsius and should be maintained throughout the treatment period. You need to follow the required temperature or all your efforts in the water bath canning food will be wasted.

Fruits, treats, fruit jellies, pickles, jams, butters, jams and acidified tomatoes and figs are suitable for the method of Canning in a water bath. Choosing the best fresh fruit is a factor considered in canning food. Fresh fruits affect the quality of your preserved foods. Fruits must first be pre-cooked before wrapping them in jars. This is called the hot packing method during the packing of raw or raw fruits and vegetables is called the cold packing method. Not all vegetables can be processed directly in the canning of the water bath like tomatoes and figs. First you need to put commercial acid on these vegetables before you can treat it under the bath method.

Water bath canning can be done easily at home for the necessary equipment in water bath canning can be improvised, simple and economical. It is not true that this method is difficult to use, because all procedures are easy to follow.

Here are these simple basic steps in Canning wate, to really understand this method:

1. Collect only fresh fruit, without imperfections.

2. Wash, dry and sterilize tools and equipment.

3. Prepare all the ingredients, cut, peel and pre-cooked.

4. Pack the food in canned jars and make sure that there are no air bubbles before sealing.

5. Boil the jars in water at a temperature of 100 degrees Celsius.

6. Cool the jars for 12-24 hours after the boiling process.

7. Test the seal of the jars before storage in a cool, dark and dry place.

8. Labelling of jars of information such as content and dates for the detection of deterioration.

Water bath canning is the safest method of storing food in your own home, because there are no procedures that are difficult to follow and easy to remember. The equipment is mainly used in your kitchen as you do not need to buy it.

That is why it is said that this is the cheapest method of canning food.

Pressure Canning Means Food Dyes and Food Coloring Are Out of Your Life

If you have problems with store-bought foods that contain food dyes or food dyes, pressurized canning of fresh products can really help them get out of your life. It doesn't seem to matter which brand you buy, most food manufacturing companies add these to make the food looks more appetizing in their canning process. Not only can this create health problems, but also commercial canned foods lack nutrients because they are too processed.

Food dyes and food dyes have been linked to a wide range of diseases, some of which are just irritations and others that are life-threatening. Everything from mild allergies to tumors and chromosomal lesions, can occur when ingested or even simply in contact with the skin. To reduce the possibility of any of these types of health problems, caning under pressure is a workable solution that anyone can pursue for a better life.

Canning under pressure is the preferred means of canning at home. It has been shown to have fewer problems with bacteria than water baths, which means that your foods will be safer for a longer period of time. You will not have to worry when you open a pot of green beans, soup or peaches for your family that there may be bacteria present that could make you sick. Following the instructions is all you need for nutritious foods that still have all their nutrients, flavor and wonderful natural color.

While it may seem less expensive to simply use a water bath to do your canning at home, pressure canning will be convenient faster in the long run. One of the biggest problems with water baths is that the seal does not always put well and then there is a bacterial growth that ferments or otherwise spoils the food making all the hard work a waste. Using a preservative under pressure, you practically eliminate this possibility, and your canned food will remain pure and ready to eat, and also have a longer shelf life. In addition, the use of a preservative under pressure is much faster than the use of a preservative in a water bath.

If you are looking for a great alternative that removes problematic food dyes and food dyes from your diet, pressure canning is the way to go. Despite the initial cost of the preservative, you will spend much less money on medications, doctor's appointments, and you will see more money in your savings account only with a few years, especially if you choose to make your products from your garden.

Save Money by Canning Food at Home

In an effort to reduce food expenses, many families choose to save money by storing food at home. An uncertain economy combined with an increase in the cost of living has forced many people to reconsider their spending habits and come up with a plan to be more frugal with their money. By growing and preparing your own food, you can reduce costs without compromising quality, taste or nutrition.

While canning your own food may seem like a lot of work, it's actually a time-saving effort since the hours invested today will make it easier to prepare meals all year round. Storing fruits, vegetables and even meat, you can store on your pantry and enjoy a variety of options, at a fraction of the cost. Buying the necessary supplies requires a modest initial cost, but your return on investment will far exceed your initial expenditure. The benefits of canning your own food are many and include the following.

1. A sense of pride and self-confidence. When you can take care of yourself without depending on the market or the economy, you feel a sense of security.

2. Viability. Growing and preparing your own food allows you to be your supermarket. There is no longer any need to worry about seasonal increases in prices, availability or food shortages.

3. Eat healthy. Canning fruits and vegetables a few hours after harvesting allows you to maintain as much nutrition as possible. In addition, trying to adhere to a budget, many people will buy substandard and less nutritious food.

Having several healthy options available, you can avoid prepackaged or unhealthy meals.

4. Free Chemical food. When you grow your food, you control both the chemicals sprayed and the preparation processes used. You can enjoy the taste and health benefits without the side effects of harmful pesticides or preservatives.

5. Reduce food costs. The purchase of seeds and plants involves an initial cost, but with proper care, the yield can be extremely high. Canning your own food allows you to become a saver rather than a spender, helping you reduce food costs by hundreds of dollars a year.

6. Affordable gifts. Decorate your pots and give them to friends, teachers or neighbors. Recipients will really appreciate your care, and your gift budget will benefit.

Although canning food may seem difficult, it's really quite simple. And there are several easy-to-follow guides that will provide you with step-by-step instructions, safety tips and useful recipes. Using either canning water bath or pressure canning, you can store your shelves with virtually anything.

For standard meals, you can prepare fruits, vegetables, meat and fish. Or spice up your menu by storing soups, sauces, gravy, chili, jams and even dairy products. Even if you do not have a garden, you can buy local and seasonal products or visit agricultural markets and meat suppliers to buy large quantities at a reasonable price. And all your work will pay off when you can open a couple of jars and prepare a quick, but nutritious and delicious meal on a busy winter day.

Uses For Used Canning Lids

Since it is dangerous to use one lid can used to seal the other jar, what to do with all the lids used?

This may not seem like a big deal to the casual preservative who sets up a couple of batches of tomatoes, jelly and jam each year.

If you get into the habit of holding a lot of things, you'll end up with a serving lot as a lid.

Instead of throwing them in the trash and adding to our dump problems, here are ten creative ideas for reusing used lids:

1. Mobile

Spray paint the lids bright colors. Drill a hole in each lid about 1/4 inch from the edge. Attach the rope to the lid, and then to the hook.

2. Matching game

Create a matching game. Print two of each letters, numbers, animal images, shapes, colors, characters, etc. cut out the elements and paste them on one side of the lid.

3. Wind chimes

Drill a small hole near the edge wide enough to pass the rope. Release the rough edges as the tip created while boring through the lid. Chain them together at different levels, but close enough for them to touch each other. As an option, you can paint the lids in different colors before assembling them.

4. Baby toy

Drill a small hole near the edge wide enough to pass the rope. Release the rough edges as the tip created while boring through the lid.

Use a tape or string to tie the lids together. Do not use rusty lids or paint them. Paint can flake.

5. Scarecrow

Polish the lids with # 0000 steel wool to give them a beautiful shine.

Hang them with string around the garden to keep birds away.

6. Fridge magnets

Print family photos. Cut them to fit the lid. Paste the picture on the lid and a small magnetic plate on the back of the lid.

They make great gifts for Christmas, birthday and grandparents.

7. Mixture in a jar

Assemble the dry mixture for a favorite family recipe (cookies, cake, beans with bacon, etc.). Discount retailers sell pots at a lower cost. Fill the jars with the dry mixture seal with the lid and the used Canning ring.

8. Storage Of Dry Goods

The lids used work well to seal mason jars filled with dry pasta, sugar, flowers, noodles, etc. you don't need a vacuum seal, just enough of a seal to keep dust and awnings away.

9. Christmas Yard Art

Drill or drill two small holes on the ends. Spray paint or polish the lids. Filament string. Another idea is to create a garland with drop-down lists of 3-5-7 of the main stream.

10. Christmas decorations

Create a set of Christmas ornaments from the lids by punching different patterns in the lid. Be creative by punching patterns such as snowmen, snowflakes, Santa Claus, Christmas tree, Cross, etc. take the lace and glue it on the outer circumference of the lid.

Canning Chicken Breast

When it comes to having a variety of emergency foods stored for potential survival purposes, meat is traditionally the hardest to accumulate. You can buy chicken, ham and Turkey in small-sized tuna cans, but believe me, they do not compare at all with the taste and quality of canned chicken breast.

If you have never tried the taste of canned chicken breast at home, you miss a fabulous treat. Canned chicken is usually more tender and moister than normal chicken, and in addition to its delicious taste, the finished product is usable for a large number of soups, stews, salads or simply as a hot plate.

Not only is it a good survival tactic to have a lot of canned chicken in the pantry, but it also saves you a trip to the local grocery store or the hassle of having to pay the usual retail price for cans. I have three or four dozen commercial versions stored in my emergency food stores and believe me, they were not cheap at all. Homemade versions are also a convenient source of chicken when you need to create a last-minute meal in no time.

There are several ways you can prepare your canned chicken ranging from using your meat for Marsala chicken to the ever popular chicken noodle soup. Chicken is a low-fat food, which has a minimum level of cholesterol, making it an exceptionally good choice for those in who appreciate their health. If you address a diet, eating chicken is definitely in your interests as it is low in calories and high in protein.

A few tips are in order when you prepare for your chicken breasts. First look at the newspaper and grocery ads and buy your your chicken when it's on sale. The bone in the chicken is Cheaper no problem, you can still it for your canning, but if you buy your your chicken without the skin, you can save yourself the trouble of stripping the breasts only.

Often you can judge the yield because one pint jar will contain about 1 1/2 of the seychelles size chicken breasts. Most modern pressure boxes can comfortably hold 8 pints per load. Be sure to keep the chicken meat fresh to'at that you some time ready to start the canning session.

Before starting the canning session, wash all jars, rings and lids in a dishwasher or boiling water. Some people argue that since the temperature in the pressure cooker will be about 235 degrees, you do not need to sterilize separately, but I like to be mistaken on the safety side when it comes to Canning. In both cases, they must be impeccably clean. Inspect all pots for chips or notches. Anything that can possibly interfere with an effective vacuum seal will lead to spoilage of food.

Add two pints of water to your pressure vessel and make sure the holder is properly seated at the bottom of it. It's finally time to remove the chicken from the refrigerator and start the session. Thoroughly wash the chicken breasts, very carefully removing the skin and any noticeable fat. The golden rule for meat processing is that it must be lean without fat otherwise you will encounter interference with good tightness.

To begin with, first fill a kettle with water and bring to a boil. Place the pressure preservative on the stove and return to medium heat.

When you wrap the meat in pots, it should be warm. Then place the chicken breasts in a large saucepan to which a small amount of water was added. Cook the breasts until they are almost done, then remove from heat and let cool for a few minutes.

At this point, you will have to work very quickly to keep the meat warm. Cut each breast into parts that fit the jar with a knife and fork. You can add a small variety by mixing large and small pieces in the same jar.

After placing the pieces of chicken breast in the first pot, set it aside and move on to the next to ' Til all the pots are completely filled. Do not pack the pots too well with the chicken, you want to leave room for the broth to fill the jar. Always leave an inch of head space in each of the buildings for expansion.

After filling all the jars with chicken, put ½ teaspoon of salt in each pint in the process of processing and be sure to also distribute the liquid in the jars. Finally, take the boiling water and fill each jar to the mark of an inch.

Never add too much liquid or there will be a leakage of liquid. Prick the mixture with a spoon to make sure that all air bubbles are removed. With a damp cloth wipe around the tops of the jars to clean the food and that put the lids with rings on the jars, being careful not to overtighten.

Put the jars in the pressure preservative and replace the machine cover.

Process according to the production instructions and drain the preservative for at least 10 minutes after the steam begins to escape from the vent. Add the ventilation cover to the box and you're almost done.

Keep an eye on the pressure gauge to ensure smooth flow. Under the processing of chicken meat is will result in deterioration while overcooking degrades both flavor and texture. Cook for about 75 minutes, then turn off the heat and drop the pressure naturally. Remove the vessels when the pressure drops properly and let them cool down.

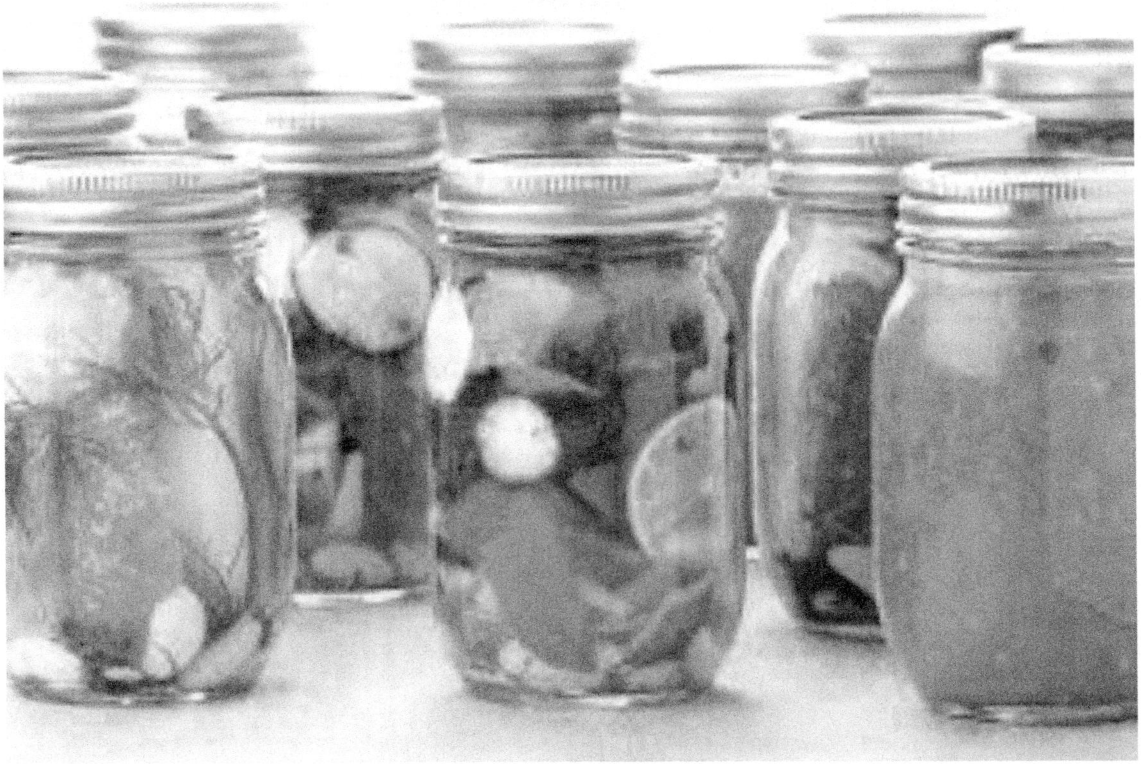

Kind reader,

Thank you very much. I hope you enjoyed the book.

Can I ask you a big favor?

I would be grateful if you would please take a few minutes to leave me a gold star on Amazon.

Thank you again for your support.

Anne Duval

Printed in Dunstable, United Kingdom